The Remarkable Extraordinary Vagina People

By
Everald Thomas

MAPLE
PUBLISHERS

The Remarkable Extraordinary Vagina People

Author: Everald Thomas

Copyright © 2024 Everald Thomas

The right of Everald Thomas to be identified as author of this work has been asserted by the author in accordance with section 77 and 78 of the Copyright, Designs and Patents Act 1988.

First Published in 2024

ISBN 978-1-83538-386-5 (Paperback)
    978-1-83538-387-2 (Hardback)
    978-1-83538-388-9 (E-Book)

Book Cover Design and Book Layout by:
    White Magic Studios
    www.whitemagicstudios.co.uk

Published by:
    Maple Publishers
    Fairbourne Drive, Atterbury,
    Milton Keynes,
    MK10 9RG, UK
    www.maplepublishers.com

INDEX

Preface 4

Chapter 1 – It's A Raw Deal 6

Chapter 2 – Fathers...Are You Okay With What Your Daughters Have to Endure With Men? 15

Chapter 3 – The False Claim of the Penis Power! 22

Chapter 4 – What if the Shoe Was on the Other Foot? .. 30

Chapter 5 – What Do Men Have to Lose? 38

Chapter 6 – I've Heard That Saying So Many Times! It's Not Easy Being A Woman! 47

Chapter 7 – Men Who Know Better – Why Are You Silent? 55

Chapter 8 – A Mother's Tears 61

Chapter 9 – Get Your Chisel Out And Start Chip Away At It 70

Chapter 10 – Gents...Time to Rip That Plaster Off! 77

Chapter 11 – Women Shaping The Future 85

Chapter 12 – Championing Social Justice 98

Chapter 13 – Sisterhood: Resilience And Strength 107

Chapter 14 – Who Gave Men The Right In The First Place? 114

Chapter 15 – The Price of Liberation! 120

Preface

In a world where progress and modernity are celebrated, it is disheartening to acknowledge that the shadows of discrimination, sexism, and chauvinism continue to loom large over the lives of countless women. This book serves as a poignant reminder of the harsh realities that many women face on a daily basis, as they navigate a landscape rife with prejudice and inequality.

The stories within these pages are not merely narratives; they are testaments to the strength, resilience, and unwavering spirit of women who confront and challenge the status quo. From subtle microaggressions to overt acts of violence, the spectrum of injustices faced by women is vast and insidious. Yet, in the face of adversity, women continue to rise, to speak out, and to demand change.

As we delve into the pages of this book, we are confronted with uncomfortable truths and stark realities. It is a call to action, a plea for empathy and a reminder that the fight for gender equality is far from over. Each story shared here is a battle cry, a plea for justice and a testament to the enduring power of the human spirit.

May this book serve as a catalyst for reflection, conversation and action. May it inspire us to stand in solidarity with women everywhere, to amplify their voices and to dismantle the systems of oppression that seek to silence them. Together, let us strive for a world where all women and girls are treated with dignity, respect and equality.

Chapter 1

It's A Raw Deal

When I write, it helps me to repair myself. It holds me to self-reflection and serves as a roadmap for my personal growth.

The next time you hear the phrase: "That's a Raw Deal" - remember Mom! There's a rib in my body which haunts me to the core, and I feel it will linger with me until I die. I cannot emphasize sufficiently how the Adam's rib story is the most difficult concept for me to grasp in terms of logical comprehension. It poses one of the greatest perplexities for me admittedly. How could I let this happen as a grown adult, I don't know!

This narrative raises many questions for me about the portrayal of gender roles and the overall general purpose of humanity. The idea that a woman was created from a man's rib perpetuates a narrative of female inferiority straight away. Ultimately, how you interpret and relate to religious stories is a personal

matter, and it's perfectly valid to approach them with an open mind and explore alternative interpretations that resonate with you on a deeper level if you find it difficult to relate to the story in a literal sense.

My view of this is - the reliance on such a mythological explanation for the existence of women undermines the complexity and diversity of human creation, reducing it to a simplistic and patriarchal account that fails to acknowledge the equality and autonomy of all individuals. I have found more compelling evidence to support the notion that women gave birth to men rather than the belief that she originated from the rib of a man. The natural process of childbirth seems more plausible to me than the symbolic story of "rib creation".

In fact, every day without fail we see her giving life to all the "Adams". And as we speak at this moment, I can guarantee you that a few Adams just plopped out of her womb, rubbing their eyes, looking at the breast and screaming out for milk. And the ironic part is, she probably just gave birth to a few disobedient, wife-beating sons who unsurprisingly grow up cursing their mothers.

Unfortunately, these abusive and controlling behaviours from men have become harmful norms in our society that we wrestle with on a daily basis. It is sad to say that this anti-feminist hostility is justified and normalised today in many cultures. Some men have even employed savage tactics to maintain that control.

However, we must push to establish respect, equality and empowerment of our women regardless of the significant resistance and backlash we face. We have to help shift these norms and beliefs by encouraging more critical thinking and aim to develop a more inclusive society where the unpleasant chauvinism and ingrained prejudices against women have no place.

This is a bad smell called sexism, and these types of opinions and bigotry are reinforced and perpetuated through education, religion, the media and other social institutions. The belief in male superiority has deep historical roots, and understanding this historical context is essential for challenging and dismantling these beliefs.

We must continue to strive for a more equitable society and understand profoundly that gender is a social construct, and it doesn't imply superiority or inferiority. We need to foster a worldwide culture of fairness, knowing that every human being born (regardless of gender) has no pervasive greatness over another. This deep-seated desire for superiority is like an infection that lives in the head. Every single one of us are all moulded and developed in the remarkable uterus of a woman.

And oh! before I forget - this fully loaded journey which generally takes 9 months is men's first recognised life insurance policy on earth. This is a binding contract between you and mummy, which is not paid out with money but with love. It also holds the obligation of your existence to her on this earthly plane. This obligation is rooted in the love, care and the selfless sacrifices she makes for us throughout our lives, regardless of our achievements and failures.

For those who are lucky to have a wonderful bond with their mums or good step-mums, you can undoubtedly testify that they are often the pillars of strength during difficult times. Similar to how an insurance policy provides a safety net for unforeseen circumstances to safeguard our future, our mothers are the sanctuary of a safe listening ear, whether it be heartbreaks, disappointments or setbacks. Mummy's emotional support often carries a miraculous healing that strongly marks victory in the face of adversity. Her economic participation is also essential for the growth and stability of communities and nations as a whole.

Recognising and honouring a mother's worth is a key part of fulfilling our obligation to her, as the level of her devotion and commitment is precious and priceless and beyond calculable. It provides wisdom and support as we navigate through the complexities of life. There are no words to describe how invaluable mothers are in shaping our world and ensuring our well-being while we grow. We repay our gratitude by honouring them with love, respect and appreciation for the beautiful gift of life they have given us.

This misguided and brainwashed concept of men having inherent dominance over females has brought nothing but long societal struggles and painful injustices for our women, hence, they are the product of the Raw Deal. These historical biases and mistreatments are countless and surprisingly still in continuance today.

However, women have come a long way from being denied the freedom of even speaking over men, being forbidden to pursue education and careers and declined the right to vote - not to mention owning properties which was a no-go zone in almost every society. They were considered to be the property of their husbands or their fathers and therefore did not have legal rights to own anything in their name.

In the United States, for example, married women were legally unable to own property until the mid to late 19th century when the Married Women's Property Acts was passed in various states, and there were similar restrictions in other parts of the world on women's property rights. While progress has been made in many areas, there are still significant cultural barriers that need to be addressed.

Today we give thanks for our "Women's Rights Movement"; even though it should simply be "Human Rights" without prejudice, but despite its numerous challenges, it has become a dynamic movement of success. They've achieved much in a short period.

Started in 1848 by two of our astounding women, Elizabeth Cady Stanton and Lucretia

Mott. These courageous mothers stood up for the advocacy of women's suffrage, giving them the right to vote in elections in what is known as the Seneca Falls Convention in the United States, which is often considered the birth of the Women's Rights Movement. Their pivotal roles in organising this convention alongside other women like Susan B. Anthony have challenged the common customs and laws that discriminate against women and set the foundation for future generations of feminists and activists today. Their beliefs, backgrounds and strong upbringings shaped their views, which led them to draft the Declaration of Sentiments which echoed the Declaration of Independence and called for women's equality.

I couldn't be more proud of our brave warrior Queens who rose against the misogynistic status quo, which was a gruelling task to undertake.

Moving forward (even though the list of discriminations is boundless), much advancement has been made in many areas and numerous successful women have reached the pinnacles of their respective fields, proving that gender is not a limiting factor.

But even then, there's much more that needs to be done as the fight for gender equality is ongoing. Society still seeks to associate leadership with masculinity, even though studies have shown that women tend to excel in empathy, social skills and emotional intelligence which are crucial in many aspects of life, including leadership, teamwork and relationships - of which many men today still struggle to accept because it brings significant changes and challenges to their traditional gender roles and causes discomfort. Therefore, they find it terrifying to accept the rise of independent women.

I have found that too many Raw Deals are being down poured on our women due to gender stereotypes when our women should be upheld as the sacred womb of creation. It's important to note that her Raw Deal is always at the end part of that stick, which carries the brown sticky bit. You know what I mean.

Chapter 2

Fathers...Are You Okay With What Your Daughters Have to Endure With Men?

E very father-daughter relationship is unique.

It is fair to say that good, caring dads typically want their daughters to grow up in a world where they are treated with respect, equality and love. Many fathers strive to raise their children, especially their daughters, to be confident and capable individuals and also empower them to manoeuvre and challenge the society's norms and expectations. They work to instil values of gender equality, empathy and wisdom in their daughters. They're always having open and honest conversations with them about men, helping them to understand what constitutes a respectful, healthy and loyal relationship. Every wise father wants his little girl to be happy, so he would teach his daughter self-worth, self-respect, encourage her to develop a strong sense of self-esteem and to believe in her abilities. He also keeps an eye on her relationships and social interactions and is aware of who she spends time with and how they treat her, and always encourages her to trust her instincts.

A well-thinking dad would make his daughter aware of sexism and relationship abuse and make sure she understands what it is, and how it can manifest in different forms so she can recognise it.

As a father, one of my greatest responsibilities is to sit my daughters down on occasions and educate them on these sensitive topics with care and concern, urging and encouraging them to recognise these issues and stand up for themselves. It is crucial to stress the importance of identifying these signs and not tolerating any form of discrimination or disrespect. It is even more urgent to discuss the topic of relationship abuse (and the different forms it can take, whether physical, emotional or verbal) delicately; to stress that no one ever has the right to mistreat her or make her feel unsafe or unworthy.

Make sure she absorbs your words and acknowledges the gravity of the subject matter, reassuring her that she should never hesitate to speak up if she ever feels like something is wrong, knowing that you will always be there to support her unconditionally.

With that vulnerable, yet empowering exchange, it effectuates a vital bond between a father and his daughter which deepens and is strengthened by a shared understanding and a commitment to navigating life's challenges together. You should make sure that your conversation has planted the seeds of resilience and self-worth in your daughter that will guide her on her journey ahead.

It is because of this high importance of the father and daughter emotional bond that men should advocate against this brutal tradition and promote inclusivity to the fullest extent to stop the devaluation of women. Recognising that gender inequality is interconnected with other forms of discrimination, such as class, race and sexuality and including physical abuse, is paramount to understanding these intersecting systems of oppression.

Each time any of my daughters complained about an abuse with their partners, whether it be deceit, maltreatment or manipulation, my ghost turns into criminal mode instantly. Even though I stay in control of my feelings, my ghost wants to grab two balls and rip them out on impulse. I know these are irrational thoughts and it's never an intelligent action to take, which is why we shift the brain and not allow ourselves to succumb to them but stay in control of our thoughts. But for any father who loves and cares about his family, this will evoke strong emotions and requires sensitivity and tactful intelligence.

As a father, watching your daughter suffer at the hands of another man is a torment unlike any other. The depths of despair and helplessness that consumed you is unfathomable. Every cry of anguish from your beloved daughter pierces through your heart like a dagger, leaving you with a trail of agony and rage. For me, the mere thought of someone daring to lay a hand on, or mentally abuse my precious child, ignites a fire within me. And this fire is fuelled by a father's primary instinct to protect his own.

So instantly the man responsible for causing my daughter's pain has become the visible form of all that is wrong with the world. All the male supremacists, the narcissists, the controlling bullies and chauvinistic toxic personalities are before my eyes. A despicable monster deserving of nothing but wrath and retribution. Yet, amidst the simmering anger of my temper, is an overwhelming sense of failure of a profound sorrow that weighs on my soul. The realization that I cannot shield my daughter from every harm, and I cannot erase the scars inflicted upon her, fill me with immense grief and regret. So, it makes a father grapple with his emotions and seek solace in silence, in the dark hours of the night. He finds himself whispering promises of support to his daughter in a relentless pursuit of justice. This is why inequalities against women must be taken down to pieces.

A father seeing his daughter suffer at the hands of another man is a test of strength and resilience. This is a battle fought not with fists, but with the heart. It's a complex mix of emotions that includes sadness, intense anger and a strong desire to protect and support your children. Just imagine a father seeing his daughter in pain and distress; it instantly triggers an impulsive reaction to intervene and protect her from further harm. It is an incredibly difficult and heartbreaking position for a father to be in. Seeing his daughter being violently abused by another man like himself is a deeply distressing and challenging situation to deal with. You'd be surprised by the strength of your feelings.

It is also extremely significant for you as a father to believe your daughter if she discloses abuse to you, and you should prioritise her safety above anything else and offer her reassurance that it is not her fault because it is a long standing systematic pattern of behaviour that has its roots anchored in years of history. It is also important to remember that the mental aspect of this abuse is a long and arduous journey, and she will have to go through the healing process of recovery.

This is why every man should give their unwavering support for this moral change. It is us, men, who ultimately hold the key and the handle of this ruthless knife; our women still hold the sharp double-edged blade in their bare hands and they have been mutilated a great number of times with it, each time an arrogant man decides to pull that handle.

There's a lot that needs to be uprooted, as this dogmatism is deeply intertwined with centuries-old systems of power and privilege where men have been predominantly in positions of authority and influence, shaping societal behaviour and structures to cater to their advantage. This well-established patriarchy has preserved a culture where women are often demoralised and repressed. Patriarchy is fundamentally about power and control, with men traditionally holding more power and influence over women in society. It has had a destructive impact on the human family for thousands of years. The destructive effects are evident in the prevalence of gender-appropriate crimes, limiting access to the overall progress for women and the determination upheld to keep it this way, which I find even more unsettling.

This task of eradication in the war against discrimination and prejudices is a community effort. We all have to tear down this trend of abuse together, which also comes with trauma and an emotional impact. The normalisation of violence against women should have no place in today's world and everything should be done to prevent its continuation across generations.

Chapter 3

The False Claim of the Penis Power!

I have been on this planet for over 3026 weeks, and I've always had this conflicting feeling and intrusive curiosity of wanting to understand the reasoning behind this masculine supremacy over women. It has always been a floating thought jumping up and down in the back of my mind. Throughout my entire life, our women, who are our Queens, our Sisters and the Mothers of our children have always been referred to universally as the second-class, lower grade species to men.

They are considered the inferior creation by "God" according to untold religious literatures. This degradation and denigration is a virile illusion stuck in tradition from way back in the dim and distant past! The ignorance and self-convinced rhetoric have overinflated men's egos for generations to the point of excessive madness. Our mothers have always been the fabric of this lifelong "fight for equal justice".

They keep having to prove themselves in every step of their earthly life under the Penis Power.

Take a look at marriage, a very sacred bond between a man and a woman, yet in some cultures it is extremely lawful to marry numerous wives, but the wife can only have the one husband. Is someone going to tell me that this is not pure greed and selfishness? My friend "D", who I've known for years, told me that he has over 40-odd brothers and sisters on his dad's side because his dad married a truckload of wives, and the worst part is, he doesn't know all of his siblings. So here we have an open gap of probability, where it's possible he himself could one day end up having kids with one of his siblings without knowing ("D" I'm not putting the bad mouth on you bro, 'cause this would be tragic for anyone, but be careful out there).

Things like this can have a serious and damaging impact on a lot of people, depending on their mental strength, all because of Mr "Greedy Who Wants Plenty", exercising his self-convinced rights to have it all for himself but his twenty seven and more wives are not allowed to have even a lettuce on the side because she's subservient to him, all because she was indoctrinated to believe so.

This historical polygamy practice where a man has multiple wives is the long-standing form of unequal gender domination, and there are strict rules and norms that dictate that while a man may have multiple wives, each wife is expected to be exclusive to him and not allowed to have relationships with any other men. This dynamic can create a power imbalance within the family structure, where the man holds authority over multiple wives who are expected to be faithful solely to him. The wives may not have the freedom to pursue relationships outside of the marriage, while the men do have the privilege of seeking additional partners with their insatiable appetites.

This unequal arrangement can have various implications for the wives involved. They experience feelings of isolation, jealousy and insecurity as they are restricted in their personal relationships, while their husband is free to engage with multiple partners. Furthermore, the lack of freedom of independence in choosing their own relationships can lead to emotional distress and a sense of being controlled or oppressed.

This inherited delusive bone of machoism has continued to reinforce a negative traditional power dynamic between men and women.

What I have come to realise in retrospect, is that men don't really gain anything valuable from this false claim of manliness except for satisfying his ego. Instead, it needs to be understood that the pressure men face to conform to these macho ideals have caused enormous constraints and anxiety on their mental health. In fact, these expectations on men can be very detrimental when he's pressured to adapt to these traditional male stereotypes, especially if they do not align with his true self. This leads to internal conflicts and distress which result in toxic masculinity.

One of the slogans under the Women's Rights Movement was "My Body, My Rights" and it is one that is very much unchallenging within the Human Rights public sphere. This empowering mantra celebrates the autonomy and freedom of women to make decisions about their own bodies. It champions the fundamental principle that every single individual has the right to control their body and wellbeing. And so with every woman, she alone has full rights to control and make decisions about her body without interference or coercion from others, including the government, healthcare providers or even family members. In my view, laws and policies that are now in place to protect women's rights over their own bodies without discrimination or barriers, should be more liberal and powerfully reinforced as they're very limiting. The same way men have the rights not to be dictated to when it comes to their body in general, the same should apply to all women and girls essentially.

It is important to recognise that women's rights to their own bodies is a global issue and women in different parts of the world may face different stumbling blocks when it comes to making decisions about their bodies. This is one fundamental right that continues to be debated and challenged in so many different parts of the world, and sadly it is way at the back of the agenda for a lot of countries. Surprisingly there doesn't seem to be any urgency to change in certain places.

I believe it is our duty as responsible adults to educate and protect this TikTok generation from this infectious gender inequality and live a life of example, showing them evidence of what we expect from them by being a positive role model. Starting early with the education is crucial for changing the current tide of this thorn of unfairness in our society. They should be taught how to speak as language shapes attitudes; using respectful and inclusive language is essential. Adults should lead by modelling respectful behaviour and demonstrate empathy and equality, setting a positive role for young people.

These strategies are important to implement, and it must be emphasised that gender justice benefits everyone and brings an equal harmonious balance to the planet on a whole. Peace will never be achieved when gender discrimination is rife in our society, as all this achieves is constant pain and hardship for our women who are the victims.

So let us appreciate our grandmothers, daughters, wives and our sisters and stop dishing out pitiful insults of hope to the Goddesses of our planet. By empowering our women, we are more likely to get an investment in families, social units and an overall development in the society, as women bring unique perspectives and ideas to the table, stimulating innovation and creativity in various fields.

Implicit bias is another parasite which is subtle and dangerously damaging, because we hold these prejudices unknowingly in our subconscious feelings due to influences and indoctrinations throughout our lives. We are unaware how these subconscious perceptions affect our decision making on others.
Everyday there's some form of unconscious discrimination being exercised, and that poses significant dangers to individuals and society on a whole.

When these discriminatory behaviours are unleashed within our society, they can promote systemic inequalities and marginalise certain groups. One has to be mindful how easily and rapidly these things trickle down, as before you know it, it affects all sorts of things like stifling overall performance in many areas as well as eroding trust and understanding.
Implicit bias is so brutal that it even gives rise to legal injustices among judges, jurors and other law enforcement officials, which leads to unfair treatment within the criminal justice system. It operates invisibly and is happening unconsciously in our brain, which is why it is so menacing.

Unfortunately, most of these imbalances are transferred to our women every moment of the day. We have to do everything to initiate fair-mindedness and equality among each other, which is why it is so important to deconstruct the mentality of this Penis Power illusion. The concept of this illusion operates on the fallacious assumption that the biological differences between men and women innately result in masculine superiority and control over all women. This belief has been historically used to justify the banishing of women's rights and independence, limiting their opportunities in society.

This so-called "penis power" is a destructive force that gave rise to a cycle of oppression and allows the prolonging of gender inequality to seep into various aspects of our communities, giving men privileges at the expense of women's liberty and power. This harmful myth must be confronted eyeball-to-eyeball and repelled, with the aim of collapsing all the systems that uphold it.

Chapter 4

What if the Shoe Was on the Other Foot?

Wh` `hat if we should flip the script, exploring a world of Reversed Male Dominance?

That shoe wouldn't fit because the chauvinistic male wouldn't try it on; he knows the pain of the squeeze on the little toe. It's that laughable!

Let's delve into a hypothetical scenario where the traditional power structures are reversed, and women exhibit chauvinistic attitudes towards men. Just imagine a society where women hold all the powers and privileges and men are systematically oppressed, as women exhibit dominant behaviours, belittling and undermining men based on their gender. They could be justifying their actions by claiming that they carried man in their womb for 9 months and nurtured him from a baby to his transitional phase of adolescence and beyond, as seen in many cases. Therefore, men should be subordinated to her and prepare to face marginalisation, discrimination and the full content of the gender prejudice package.

I can see that it would be painfully difficult to even form a mental picture of the male dominance being flipped on its head, leading to systemic barriers for men to access opportunities, workplace discrimination, low pay gap compared to women, lack of access to education due to gender identity, only allowed to have one wife while the women can choose multiple husbands - the restrictive list can go on and on. How do you think men would thrive in a biased environment like this?

I believe men in a society characterised by reversed male chauvinism as described above may struggle with their emotional well-being and mental health due to societal pressures, leading to issues such as anxiety, depression, and low self-worth. I have no doubt that if these roles were to truly reverse, a lot of men would struggle with the pressure to be more open with their emotions and vulnerable in their interactions. This could be bumpy for so many men who have been socialized to suppress their emotions and uphold a facade of masculine strength. If the role of caregiving and household responsibilities was to transfer over to the men's side, a lot of men would be bald because they would be pulling out their hair every day. It would be an interesting experience, finding themselves facing new and difficult tasks in balancing work and family responsibilities, as well as dealing with societal stereotypes around what it means to be a man.

We always feel the need to uphold a pretence of morality, even at the expense of the truth. But to actually experience the feeling of this type of prejudice being repeatedly thrust at you – it would be a completely different ball game to see how the reversal of power dynamics affects the social issues here, and how individual men would react to losing their rights and facing sexism on a daily basis. If you think you're man enough and have a strong enough backbone to handle this type of discrimination, I can tell you now, that's a pile of rotten cabbage stored in your head.

The goal of exploring this scenario is not to perpetuate divisiveness or reinforce any form of stereotypes, but to foster empathy and understanding, as well as dialogue between the groups. I am completely certain that if the shoe was on the other foot as I've said before, not one male Cinderella could handle the burning toe in that squeezing shoe. And I am saying this as a thought experiment to provoke critical thinking among yourselves. You have to put yourself in the picture frame in order to see the injustices being dished out on our women in real terms.

In the realm of human interactions, especially in the case of gender prejudices, it is clear that frustrations often rear their ugly heads when selfish desires are being attacked or thwarted. Therefore I expect men who are consumed by their own ambitions and self-serving agendas to become irate and disheartened when they hear these things echoing on a loud speaker back at them. But what is more disastrous in this situation is the inability of men to realise that these selfish, traditional roots of discriminations have led to a storm of emotional resentment, dissatisfaction and deep-seated anger for our women for centuries, all because we allow our frustrations to set in like a dark cloud when we are unable to manipulate circumstances to align our egocentric visions that we've created.

If we turn a blind eye and let this go unchallenged, it can be a bitter pill to swallow later on, leaving behind a trail of discontent and discord in its wake. We have seen these reoccurrences prolonging time and time again. It's time for us to learn that the journey of chasing selfish aspirations will only result in disappointments and lead to social unrest and ultimate discontent. There's no need to feel threatened by our women, or fear a loss of control if we get rid of the competitive mindset.

Living this short life on earth shouldn't be a competition, but because history has made men hold more power and privilege in our society, the fear of losing control or dominance is what's bothering the ego and converting the meaning - for some - as an attack on men.
But in reality, all that's happening now is our women being assertive, independent and ambitious, and if this makes you feel insecure about your own abilities and status then it's because you've cultivated a fixed mental disposition of conflict. You appear to be living a normal life, but in fact, you're striving to be the boss over the female species. At the same time, you're looking at life as a contest when it should be a togetherness of sharing and caring regardless of gender.

It is imperative to acknowledge that women are truly a rich tapestry of society who stand as pillars of strength and durability which is irrefutable. Their contributions, from the very foundation upon which communities thrive and flourish, are often understated and overlooked. It is essential that we not only acknowledge but also deeply respect and appreciate the invaluable role that women play in shaping our world.

From the tender embrace of a mother to the unwavering support of her friendship, women bring a unique blend of compassion, wisdom and light to every facet of life. Their capabilities and multi-sided talents know no bounds, as they excel in various professions, nurture families and champion serious issues with unswerving dedication. There are so many important contributions that our women have made to the planet. Their impact can be seen across all aspects of society, and their achievements continue to inspire and enable future generations.

That Cinderella shoe may not be able to fit the foot of any chauvinistic male due to the ingrained traditional norms which he accepts within his head. It is incumbent upon us however as men, and as the representative of the family's patriarch, to not only recognise the struggles that women face but also actively work towards disassembling the foundation that keeps the unfairness and injustices in existence.

We should build support networks, engaging men and boys as allies in the fight for gender justices and challenge those harmful benchmarks which discriminate against women's rights.

In doing so, men would also be educating themselves about these issues and the impact of discrimination and bias on women's lives. Reading books, articles, engaging in discussions and researching gender unfairness will increase understanding. There is a need to listen to women's experiences and perspectives about some of the preferential they face daily and turned up the volume of their voices by sharing their stories. She is the biggest survivor of abuse and gender-based violence, whether it be domestic violence, sexual assault or harassment - you name it, she has been through them all disproportionately. It's time for men to work alongside women as partners and celebrate their achievements wholeheartedly by uplifting their voices and honour their presence in our midst. Strive to create a world where every woman is valued, empowered and respected for the distinctive gifts she brings to the world. For in honouring and appreciating our women, we sow the seeds of a harmonious foundation of equity that is unshakable for generations to come.

I hope this hypothetical scenario of reversed male chauvinism serves as a powerful tool for understanding the damaging effects of gender-based discrimination and the need for collective efforts to dismantle oppressive ideologies. Maybe if this changing course of direction was to become the new norm, it could lead to a period of adjustment and redefinition for men. It would certainly require a shift in the mindset for sure, and a re-evaluation of what it means to be a man in a world of reversed gender roles or where gender roles are no longer strictly defined. By confronting chauvinism in all its forms and promoting respect, equality and empathy, we can create a more just and equitable world for future generations.

Chapter 5

What Do Men Have to Lose?

Absolutely NOTHING…apart from a false pride and a fictitious traditional claim of being the world boss! In fact, men have a lot more to gain by actively supporting women's rights. It would mean that we are contributing to a more just and healthier lifestyle, where men would gain personal growth and understanding which would help to develop greater empathy and awareness of the experiences and challenges faced by women, as well as help to create a more level playing field for everyone. This means we can build stronger and more equal relationships with the women in our lives, whether it be partners, family members, friends or colleagues. This can lead to more fulfilling and appropriately combined relationships based on mutual respect. So, there is absolutely nothing to lose guys. Your sense of power is not tied to your masculine traits. The seat of your power is in your efforts to rise as well as your hard work and ambition, which all sits in your brain. Showing vulnerability or weakness doesn't make you less of a man. It is simply the traits of being purely human, and nothing to do with gender Identity.

It is important that we embrace a broader definition of masculinity which includes compassion, fragility and deeper emotional intelligence, as this is likely to promote healthier attitudes towards power and identity and consequently relinquish the fear of societal stigmatism for men, which has somewhat become a burden laid down on him by traditional culture.

Let us talk about Strength in Vulnerability and why I think it's important for men to express their emotions. In a society that often equates masculinity with power and emotional suppression, there is a prevailing myth as we all know it, that men should always be strong, tough, and unyielding. However, I feel this narrow definition of masculinity can be harmful at times in reality. It is crucial to recognize that vulnerability and the willingness to show weaknesses are not signs of inadequacy, but rather, they are indicators of courage, strength, and emotional intelligence. I believe when men allow themselves to be vulnerable, in a sense, they break free from the constraints of societal expectations and open themselves up to a world of emotional authenticity and deeper connections.

By acknowledging our vulnerabilities, men demonstrate a profound sense of self-reflection, internal truth and correctness and an acceptance of our humanness. This act of self-disclosure can foster trust, affinity, and intimacy in relationships, leading to more meaningful connections with others. Moreover, embracing vulnerability can be a powerful tool for personal growth. Just think about it guys; when we allow ourselves to express our emotions and confront our weaknesses, we embark on a journey of self-discovery and self-improvement. By acknowledging and addressing vulnerabilities men can develop, believe it or not, greater self-esteem, emotional maturity and coping skills, enabling them to work through life's challenges with grace and authenticity.

Some may not agree, but I believe it is important to create a culture that encourages and celebrates men's naivety and emotional expression. By confronting so-called traditional norms of manliness and promoting a more compassionate understanding of manhood, we can empower men to embrace their emotions, seek support when needed and cultivate healthier relationships both with themselves and others. It is not a sign of weakness for men to show vulnerability or express their emotions; rather, it is a display of inner-strength and spiritual authenticity. By embracing our weaknesses, men can unlock true potential and lead more fulfilling lives in society. It is time to redefine masculinity and create a world where men feel empowered to be their most authentic selves, flaws and all.

When you think about it, this burdensome weight that men are expected to carry is becoming more increasingly apparent. From a young age, we were often taught to embody traits of strength and dominance which can be suffocating. It's like we are conditioned to believe that we must always be in control, both emotionally and physically, leading to a suppression of hidden feebleness and a denial of our own struggles. You can see that the pressure to conform to traditional masculine norms can easily result in a sense of detachment and alienation in many cases, as men fear showing any sign of weakness or deviation from the expected role. Furthermore, the expectation on men to mainly provide and protect can also place a weighty millstone around his neck, resulting in high levels of stress and anxiety as they push enormously in their roles as providers and leaders for their families and communities. It is vital to understand the weight that men carry around under the umbrella of this masculine superpower as they hardly have space to express their emotions and frailty.

Because of this, many men suffer mental health issues in silence due to this type of culture's high expectations of machoism. Some fear losing social status and privileges in society which makes them scared to burst into tears and bawl when their emotions are bruised. They think of how it will be perceived by others or expose them to judgement or ridicule. So we, men, tend to internalise everything, bottling up pain and bitterness, living a lie in public just to protect this masculine pride we inherit by tradition. Some men may even feel that their sense of self-worth and true identity is deeply connected to this kind of inflated masculinity, which challenge their self-perception and often lead to feelings of not being enough and feeling insecure if they fail to live up to these expectations.

This for me is a strong exaggerated sense of manliness. It makes some men feel like they cannot rise to their role, or that they don't have the passion to ignite their purpose as a man. This misconception is fuelled by egotism. It's a complete nonsense that is ruining precious life moments. We all have masculine and feminine energies within us regardless of what gender we are. But men tend to suppress their feminine sides in order to feel assertive and accomplished. But the truth is, men really need to tap into their feminine energies to achieve inner-balance and wholeness. By integrating these two aspects, man can enhance his ability to connect with others on a much deeper level.

There is always a need to think outside the box. It brings fresh perspectives and personal endeavours to our lives when we embrace a mindset of creative and unconventional thinking. This is where we get to self-discovery and personal maturity, as well as explore new possibilities when we step out of our comfort zone. There is no doubt that this will absolutely lead to personal fulfilment and satisfaction when we challenge ourselves and push boundaries, especially in this area of prejudice where we form unfair opinions of people, especially women.

Dudes, we ought to get real with ourselves and put the spotlight on our minds. We simply have too many inaccurate concepts about our female species and the way we want them to live, behave and breathe. We already perceive her by stereotype to be solely responsible for the household chores and childcare etc, and we want them to dress a certain way too. We treat them like little children, all because we think they are less competent and somewhat subordinate to us. We continue to underrate, box up and label our women according to the history of tradition. We generalise all women based on stereotypical assumptions. We must bring ourselves to realise that our women have individual choices and capabilities, as well as diverse desires and preferences of which they are entitled to without the approval of others, and which must be respected by men at all costs.

Women, just like men, are their own independent beings with their own unique personalities, interests and characteristics. So it is not accurate for any individual or group to have the authority to impose unjust restrictions or limitations on others based solely on their gender, because the principles of equality and human rights applies to all genders right across the globe.

We know very well that society has been structured in a way that placed men in powerful positions of authority over women for centuries, and this has never been taken on or unequivocally and rigorously challenged. Gradually it becomes the unexceptional rule that has been kept alive through various means like laws, religious beliefs and cultural standards. So here we have many complex reasons why some men may be resistant to gender equality and seek to keep women inferior, as they feel threatened by the idea of women gaining equal rights and opportunities because it opposes their traditional roles as the dominant gender. Again, some men may feel insecure about their own abilities or worth and may see this control and power over women as a way to boost their own self-esteem. This has to be eliminated in this day and age.

If there was ever a time for amplifying and centring women's voices, it's now! It can only have huge benefits and a moral impact if we start to promote, highlight and elevate her work and her worth and give credit where it's due.

Recognizing her contributions in your community and beyond will only bring together the spirit of unity and humanness that is missing. Gents don't be afraid to support women-led initiatives and back the organisations, campaigns and projects that are led by women and raise the importance of gender equality everywhere. Giving up chauvinism will lead to a happier life, thriving relationships, as well as embracing a better mental well-being for our future. Chauvinism and toxic masculinity only contribute to stress, depression and anxiety, and it is a blind and absurd devotion to a delusive loyalty we've been tied down with from tradition. Men who let go of these constraints can find themselves with a new sense of freedom and empowerment in their everyday lives as they progress.

⸺◈⟨⟩◈⸺

Chapter 6

I've Heard That Saying So Many Times! It's Not Easy Being A Woman!

In terms of physical characteristics such as chromosomes, hormones and reproductive anatomy, I am a biological man! I haven't got a female reproductive system. I understand and respect the diversity of gender identities in today's world, but I will never truly understand how it is to live as a woman.

Today my mind is open and reflecting on the life lived by my mother and our women in society. Being on this planet for so long, and from what I've seen during my adolescence growing through to manhood, is the difference in pain between the life of my mother and my father. I realised from back then, that between the two gender roles, they have been assigned different responsibilities and expectations by society's standards of which one of them is always facing ongoing and agonising pressure of an enormous magnitude too strong for the Richter scale. The thing that has become apparent and most uncomfortable to digest here, is the undeniable fact that the primary element of the women's struggle worldwide is solely gender based. She's accustomed to being generally affected by domestic violence, sexual assault, human trafficking, honour killings, a gender pay gap, unequal treatment in the workplace based on her gender, pregnancy discrimination, forced into child marriages at a young age often without their consent; and these are just a few examples of the continuing injustices faced by women today, all of which we have touched on before and cannot be overstated.

If I am honest, the adjectives "extraordinary and remarkable" are inadequate to describe this special human species. For what women have to endure, I know I couldn't do it. Men cannot and could not do it. We can hardly survive a toothache without turning into a 3-month-old baby, and I won't even elaborate on emotional pain like being cheated on by our partners, because unfortunately for many men, that becomes a suicide mission. We give it, but we can't take it, even if it comes with syrup and cream.

This is what I meant when I said how interesting it would be if men try to live in the role of a woman in a man's world, encountering all the systematic barriers of discrimination and harassment. The more I think about it in a sense, the more I start to believe that this would be a transformative eye-opening experience which could lead to a deepening understanding of the need for more men to engage in campaigns for gender fairness. Over and over, our women are consistently being treated with an iron fist, and many are too powerless and fearful to address it, so their burden becomes overwhelmed and the only thing to release that burden is their tears. Day by day she's wrongly accused and faces undeserved punishment. Meanwhile the power of the penis continues to roam, committing crimes against Womanity, approved by the norms of tradition, which mean they get away with it every day.

But come what may, a woman's heart seems as though it was built from a hard-wearing material called resilience despite the intense hardship it faces. She seems to be endowed with a coping mechanism that is indestructible to man. The intensity of some of the persecutions she faces means it is somewhat impossible to understand how she pulls through them sometimes, which is why she's still around today, standing unshakable.

She exhibits remarkable strength and endurance in the face of severe victimisation even when she reaches breaking point. With these obstacles and challenges in so many societies around the world, it's really hard to be a woman. But somehow it looks like the Universe has fashioned these species with toughness and durability, leaving men in "awe" each time she bounces back from the vicious setbacks.

This also proves, that while hardship can be difficult to endure, it can also shift people's perspective on life and drives us to develop a mindset of adaptability, building inner strength, growth and confidence while going through tough times. To be a breathing woman today requires courage and enormous faith to battle the sea of gender crimes waged against her. She has to keep fighting for everything from the moment that ultra scan reveals "it is a girl". If she doesn't take control of her power and her divine rights to survive from an early age, the quality of her life will be determined by the so-called ruling penis bully who thinks he has the right to jump in her decision making at any time and make personal decisions for her about her body, her looks, the type of clothing she should or shouldn't wear and how much knowledge she should have. The thing that makes it so grim is that men don't probe to understand her feelings enough or seek to inspire her when she is in a weak state. Instead, he commands and forces his opinions onto her, waving his slavery whip and chain over her head in intimidation just in case she dares to resist.

It is fair to say, from what we've witnessed, it is an unseen struggle navigating this world as a woman as it comes with its own set of distresses and objections that are often overlooked. From a young age, girls are taught to manoeuvre a society that is rampant with gender biases and miscalculations. The journey of our females is often marked by forceful efforts that are firmly established in the fabric of our society.

One of the most pervasive challenges that women face is the constant pressure to conform to social standards of beauty and behaviour. Most women, both young and old, are bombarded with images and directives that dictate how they should look, act, and speak. The pressure to meet these unrealistic standards can take a toll on a woman's self-esteem and confidence, and she can start to develop issues with body image concerns and low self-worth. In addition to public expectations around her appearance, women also face constitutional barriers in various aspects of their lives. They often find themselves tactically shuffling through male-dominated spaces where their voices are either suppressed or dismissed. These disparities protract a cycle of inequality which is difficult to break. We should insist on the essence of human rights and embrace equality.

Equality is the cornerstone of a just and fair society. It is the elementary human principle that all individuals are born naturally equal in dignity and rights. The essence of equality rests in recognising and respecting the humanity and worth of every person, regardless of their background, identity, or circumstances. The heart of equality to me is the recognition of equal nobility of all individuals, where every person deserves to be treated with fairness and consideration, regardless of socioeconomic status. Every human being possesses an innate worth and should be valued as such. Upholding the principle of equal dignity is essential for fostering mutual respect and understanding among diverse communities. Equality also entails ensuring that all individuals have the same rights and opportunities, which includes the right to life, liberty, security, education, healthcare, employment etc. Equal rights empower individuals, whether man or woman, to fulfil their potential and contribute to society in more meaningful ways. By guaranteeing the same opportunities with the essential aspect of balanced treatment for all, we create a just and fair society.

As we reflect back on our women and the journey they have travelled, it has to be said that their strong nature proves that adversity does build character, and overcoming obstacles requires individuals to think creatively and find solutions which increases their problem solving skills and improves their ability to better handle future obstacles.

Our females truly need to be honoured and admired in this arena. There should be no space in our society for such an ugly thing as gender supremacy. We are all the same human weaklings controlled by one universal breath coming in and out of our nostrils, and none of us come out of here alive regardless of how much wealth we have.

This is not only morally imperative but also a practical necessity for building a better world for present and future generation where we embrace and celebrate, as well as recognise and value the diversity of all our human experiences and the unique contributions of each individual. In doing so, we enrich our collective humanness and build stronger and more loving communities - forget about gender prejudices and thrive for the highest achievement in our lives.

⸺⸰⸰◅◆▻⸰⸰⸺

Chapter 7

Men Who Know Better – Why Are You Silent?

I just don't get it!

Where women continue to face various forms of cruelty and discrimination in our society, the silence of men on these issues remains a troubling phenomenon for me. Let us try to unpack the reasons behind this inaction in the face of women's cruelty. Despite being aware of the injustices and suffering that women experience on a daily basis, many men choose to remain silent and complicit in their inaction. This silence raises important questions about power social constructs, fear and complicity that warrant deeper exploration.

Men are often socially influenced from a young age to adhere to traditional notions of masculinity that emphasise strength and control. Expressing empathy or speaking out against injustices faced by women may be perceived as a sign of weakness or vulnerability, leading some men to stay silent to uphold their masculine identity, and that's one aspect! On the other hand, men who do speak out against women's cruelty may fear backlash or retaliation from their peers or even the perpetrators themselves. For the fear of being banished, ridiculed, or even physically harmed can be a significant barrier to men who openly addressing these issues in many cases.

Also, you cannot rule out that men, particularly those who benefit from privileges in society, may unconsciously or knowingly prolong systems of oppression that harm women. This complicity can create a sense of guilt or discomfort that makes it easier to turn a blind eye to women's suffering rather than confront their own role that continues to push these rather harmful behaviours.

It is possible that some men may simply lack a deep understanding of the experiences and challenges faced by women. Without firsthand experience or education on the realities of women's lives, it can be difficult for men to empathize with their struggles and prioritize their voices in conversations about cruelty and injustice. This silence of men is a multifaceted issue that requires introspection and active efforts to challenge existing power forces and social norms. By acknowledging the reasons behind this silence and working to dismantle the barriers to speaking out, men can play a crucial role in support for equality, justice, and respect for all.

When we examine our livity as human species and see how we can improve and enhance our collective human experience away from prejudice and gender stereotypes, we should encourage the targeting of global citizenship which would improve learning and adaptation. This also would promote understanding among diverse cultures and nations whilst striving for both personal and collective growth. Self-reflection is a crucial tool to activate, because it helps to combat ignorance and promote critical thinking of ourselves.

Men who know better are expected to lead this crusade, wearing the dignity of their mothers and daughters on their sleeves and not being muted. We are in a battle against misogynism, and we should pledge our support valiantly to gender equality and disassemble the chauvinistic mentality from among us. Men who use masculinity to dominate their women are still in the pram. They haven't really grown up yet. They're still carrying around an infantile mindset which sums up their inability to comprehend. Too many men out there today are dead jealous of their wife's progression and don't want to see them grow, and that I find demoralising and counterproductive. It explains the definition of sleeping with the enemy. They are extremely afraid of her potential and growth. These men are not in a relationship based on love and building a togetherness, they're more in a love-competition where they always want to stay ahead and keep her behind at all costs, to maintain or cover up his personal insecurities. He's afraid he might be giving up his traditional gender role, which assigned him to be the primary decision maker and breadwinner of the house, and that's not the case. Many women challenge these roles by advancing in education, careers and leadership positions and it rattles the cages of these men and makes them very uncomfortable, as if they were being castrated.

This misunderstanding or misconception about feminism and gender equalness has contributed to fear and resistance towards women's progress. Depending on the environment in which they were raised, some men have wrongly perceived this to be a threat to their own rights or status, thinking that it may shackle their abilities to achieve, and they fear being overshadowed or feel inadequate when they see women succeeding. But this is misconstrued, instead, there are so many reasons why men should feel empowered and supportive when women are excelling because "Equality" benefits everyone. When women have equal opportunities to excel, it broadens the benefits in more ways than one.

Having and displaying equality among ourselves regardless of gender can only lead to more diversity and inclusiveness in our society which will promote change and bring in more creativity and economic growth which benefits everyone.

Men and women are not in competition with each other, but should be supportive and appreciative of each other to create a more stable and harmonious society where everyone can thrive. The phenomenal thing about harmony is that it lets you communicate and work firmly towards common goals. It can also help to resolve conflicts in a healthy manner and is undoubtedly crucial for success overall.

I want to rest my hand on my heart and sincerely say, I appreciate and respect all men who recognise and acknowledge the negative impact of male supremacy in our world today. It takes courage and humility to challenge and change harmful beliefs such as those. To acknowledge one's faults and shortcomings are true signs of maturity, strength and personal growth. I salute you all, you are gentlemen of integrity. You've exhibited ethical and moral qualities and contribute positively to society, and you will in no doubt inspire others to do the same.

Be proud, wear it as a badge of honour and don't be silent.

Chapter 8

A Mother's Tears

In this chapter I want to focus mainly on men and their mothers. It's important to note that not all men have a close or loving relationship with their mothers and that saddens me, because to me, that feels like a birth-right robbery and makes my bowels weak. For those who happen to have, or have had, the luxury of a dedicated and caring mother in your life, happy are you. Perhaps you already know where I'm going to take you, but come with me!

A mother's tears can be particularly painful because they often represent deep emotions and feelings of love, sadness, worry or disappointments.

I happened to peeked around the corner sadly a few times and caught my mother crying. Sometimes she'd sit on the edge of the bed and her shoulders silently shaking from sobbing. Seeing my mother's tears for the very first time sent a pang of fear through my little heart. I was confused, cos mommy was valiant and courageous, and I used to see her as my source of comfort. Tears welled up in my eyes and I felt a very deep pain in my chest. I stood frozen, unsure of what to do. Still, I've never known or seen another woman so bravely determined.

For those who are fortunate to have her in your life, you'll always understand that memorable earthly experience. The love that most men have for their mother is a complex and unique one. The biological bond between a mother and her child is often established from the moment of birth through physical and emotional connections, such as breast feeding, comfort and care. This early bond seems to create a strong foundation for a lifelong relationship between the two. Alot of men look up to their mothers as examples of inner-strength, resilience and compassion. The unwavering support from her seems to foster a sense of security and belonging in men, which leads to a strong emotional attachment. Each time I hear the words "Unconditional Love", the picture of a mother and child flashes in my mind.

This is why I am confused and trying to unpack the double standards of this gender bigotry and how it even started.

In many cultures, mothers are always portrayed as the central figures who play a highly significant role as the matriarch of the family. Even though daddy rules physically, she monitors silently in the background. She is like magic and power. Mothers naturally master the innate emotion of nurturing and warmth and applies her duty of care with dedication and diligence. She goes to bed with all the tasks of tomorrow well planned and mentally thought through, and she does that selflessly!

In order to understand the phrase, "A Mother's Tears", you have to be connected by heart. It is often used to evoke the deep emotions felt by mothers, especially when she's worried or in distress. When her children are suffering or she senses danger around them, she's converted into something and someone extraordinary. That phrase in itself is particularly moving and poignant, because it symbolises her love and the profound emotional connection to her children.

Let's get into the tears part a bit!

When a child witnesses their mother's tears, it leaves a permanent imprint. It's like a rising volcanic eruption which is naturally inevitable to upset that child, as it goes straight to the heart strings. You recognise this as a sign of distress, vulnerability or excess pain that your mother is going through and it can be very difficult for a child to process. Can you imagine as a young boy I enter the room, I immediately sense a shift in the atmosphere. The usual warmth and cheerfulness that envelopes my home has dissipated, replaced by an unsettling tension that I could almost taste in the air. My mother who usually is the epitome of strength and perseverance, now sits on the edge of her bed with her shoulders slumped and her eyes distant and filled with water.

Confusion washes over me as I take in the sight of a very distressed mother I've never seen like this before. A knot forms in my stomach as I witness her pain. I struggle to make sense of what I am seeing and my heart starts to race. It was a very disturbing picture, and I grappled with the unfamiliar sensation of seeing my mother in such a vulnerable state. A whirlwind of questions swirled in my head, and at the same time, a sense of sadness set in, as I realize that my mother, the one who always knows how to chase away my fears and worries, is now the one in need of comfort. I wanted to reach out to my mum, to wrap her in a hug and whisper words of reassurance, but a part of me felt unsure; unsure of how to navigate this unfamiliar territory of witnessing my mother's vulnerability.

In the midst of my own turmoil, as a little boy, I clenched to a mixture of emotions – fear, sadness, confusion, and a deep-rooted desire to protect the woman who has always been my rock. Despite feeling overwhelmed by the weight of her distress, a sense of determination sparked within me, a silent promise to be there for her in whatever way I could, just as she has always been there for me.

In that moment, I was faced with a profound realisation - that even the strongest of figures in my life can falter, and that it is okay to feel scared and unsure in the face of peril. There were many odd and unusual thoughts that came crashing in my head. Many times, I think her tears was a soulful communication which provided a source of re-energised strength in her. I've seen her rise and bounce back each time after a good cry. It's like each crying session, something from that turbulence transfigured my mother into someone lighter, calmer and more powerful.

We know that mothers are always sacrificing so much for their children and her painful tears serve as a reminder of the strong bond, deep connection and emotional ties that exist within the family unit. Those men who have a loving and supportive relationship with their mothers may have a strong foundation for understanding and expressing love, and may also have a positive outlook on relationships and are more likely to treat their partners with respect and kindness. While on the other hand, men who did not have a good relationship with their mother or never had a motherly figure in their life may struggle with emotional issues, trust and intimacy in their relationships. They might find it challenging to work through passionate connections and have difficulty expressing love and empathy.

However, it is important to say that individual experiences and circumstances vary, and not all men fit neatly into these categories because many men had to use their spiritual intelligence to build a positive life for themselves and their family without a mother's presence in their youthful life. The dynamics of the mother-son relationship can be influenced by many factors including personality, cultural norms and individual experiences. Ultimately, the quality of the attachment between a mother and her child is shaped by the love, care, attention and the emotional support that the mother provides, as well as the child's unique needs and personality. My relationship with my mother was very quirky. One of the annoying things my mother always did to me - when I would get dressed for school or church, she use to use the spittle from her mouth to touch out whatever sleep residue she saw between my eyes or any dry spots on my face while she reprimanded me for not bathing myself properly.

But she was simply my Earth Goddess, and nothing could override that. Each drop of her tears witnessed were like a blade walking through my skin and I felt helpless, knowing that my mother to me was always the primary caregiver and source of my comfort and security. This can leave us troubled as kids and confused for several reasons. For instance, children are naturally empathetic and sensitive to the emotions around them. So, seeing their mother crying can trigger feelings of multiple mixed emotions in the child, whether it be sadness or helplessness, as (depending on their age) they may not fully understand the reason behind their mother's tears but can sense her distress.

The other important thing is attachment. The relationship between a child and their mother is fundamental to the child's emotional development. So, seeing the mother upset can shake the child's sense of security and stability, since the mother is often seen as that fortified strength and resolution. There is also vulnerability, because as children we rely on parents for protection and care so again seeing mummy cry, can make them feel vulnerable and exposed as they are used to their mother being the one who provides hope and reassurance. Some children may not have the emotional maturity or cognitive ability to fully understand complex emotions or situations that lead to their mother's tears, and this lack of understanding can leave them feeling very anxious and jumbled.

Let us value and honour the emotions and feelings that our mothers express through their tears, and reflect on the deep sense of love she bestows on us and the significance of her emotions. Tears are naturally a physiological response that provides emotional relief of stress and other toxins released from our bodies. Remember that a mother's tears can be a combination of love and joy too. It springs from an overwhelming feeling of happiness and pride for her children. She also sheds tears out of concern or agonizes when her child is going through a difficult time or experiencing pain or facing dilemmas. Despite the tears, a mother's strength and resilience shines through. She seems to have an ability to overcome challenges and keeps going even in the face of adversity.

We should value and respect our mother's tears of strength, because without HER there's no HIM.

Chapter 9

Get Your Chisel Out And Start Chip Away At It

I t is vital to chip away at stereotypes at all costs and promote a culture of sharing and oneness amongst ourselves. It is important we understand that acknowledgement and awareness go a long way.

First, learn about the root cause, the human impact and the manifestation of gender prejudices, and actively challenge what contributes to the continuing of this hostile tradition. It is also very important to question assumptions, because in doing so, you can dispute existing beliefs and viewpoints which can lead to deeper understandings, as well as help you to see things from different angles. This can open up the possibility for new ideas and innovative solutions.

By challenging the status quo, you can think independently and creatively which brings adaptability and flexibility in individuals away from conventional thinking, which involves following the established norms and standards that guides our thinking and behaviour.

When you question assumptions, you uncover potential errors or misconceptions and prevent making decisions based on faulty premises. We should aim to create a more welcoming and respectful environment for people of all backgrounds and identities regardless of gender. Recognising that a person's gender should not be the determining factor in how they are treated and valued is highly important and should not play a role in discussions of equality. Every individual has inherent human worth and dignity and therefore, equality should be based on the principle that all human beings deserve respect and fairness, as well as equal opportunities in spite of their gender identity. Anything that is excluding or discriminating against individuals, and is hinged on gender, goes against the principle of equality for all. Focusing on human impartiality without considering a person's gender in any way should be the mindset that every decent human being holds; otherwise, these traditional gender roles will continue to thrive and form unequal treatment based on gender norms.

I believe it is now time to examine and reflect on your own beliefs and attitudes towards gender. Understanding our own biases allows us to recognise when they might be influencing our thoughts, our actions and our decisions. We should consider where these beliefs come from and how unfair and harmful they are in today's world. Hold yourself accountable and be willing to acknowledge and take responsibility for any chauvinistic attitudes and behaviours you may exhibit. Let us learn from our mistakes gents, be apologetic when necessary, and commit to making positive changes to our behaviour.

Everyone makes mistakes, but one thing I know for sure about mistakes is that they provide valuable learning opportunities. By reflecting on them, we can identify what went wrong, understand why it happened and figure out how to avoid repeating that same error. It is crucial, not just for personal growth, but societal progress and even the advancement of human civilization on a whole.

For instance, many of our greatest inventions and advancements in human history have come as a result of trial and error, because by analysing past mistakes we can refine our approach and develop new solutions, and even push the boundaries of what was once deemed to be impossible which has now become accomplishable. And that's what we call true development, the ability to bounce back from the setbacks and failures and ultimately thrive in the face of challenges. It is an essential component of personal growth. If we look back today on some of the errors made by our ancestors in terms of inequalities and gender prejudices, it is only natural to take the sensible steps to correct these mean judgements of tradition and build an intellectually unbiased way of life for ourselves without favouritism in our modern world.

By chipping away at anything that is discriminatory, such as misogynism and male dominance, we are actually making incremental progress towards building a fair and justified society by breaking down centuries of statewide, or in fact global negative practices, where our women especially can thrive in a comfortable and balanced surroundings without fear and mental pressures within their daily lives. I believe that once there's a negative situation, it should be addressed, because negativity can snowball and worsens if left unchecked. By addressing any unfavourable situations early and consistently, you can prevent them from escalating into more serious issues. I also believe that constant exposure to negativity, such as discrimination can take a toll on a person's mental health. Dealing with these situations should be a top priority and should be dealt with in a proactive manner to build inner strength and fortitude in people, so they can lead a life of confidence and be able to extend this to their communities.

There are millions of decently honest people on the planet who are seeing this type of injustice playing out every day and finding it painstaking to watch, and I'm sure most of them are eager to do something to correct this outrageous oppression but are deterred by strong and forceful oppositions who are highly resistant to change. These forces can create significant barriers to stop any sort of change and would do anything to keep it where it is. It's quite likely they feel threatened of losing their existing power or importance, which could be some entrenched interests, such as economic incentives, sovereignty or just ideological beliefs. Whatever the reason is, for me it is illogical in this day and age, as the role of women has changed remarkably as women are now self-sufficient, well aware and financially independent. They have broken barriers in many vital areas. They have achieved immense success in almost every field over the years. They have shown exceptional courage and dedication in their respective fields, winning Nobel Prizes and shattering glass ceilings in the business world. They became influential figures in our society today, and should be thunderously applauded for being able to break free from those extremely inhumane traditional roles and expectations, knowing their historical struggle for equal rights and their fight for suffrage was painstaking amongst numerous other things.

They should continue to be supported and empowered in reaching even greater heights, to flourish and accomplish their long deserved place of equality in human history. The key thing about supporting women to excel in our world is to know that it is not just a moral duty but also a strategic investment in the future.

In a world where problems often seem insurmountable and obstacles loom large, it is crucial to uplift and empower those around us to strive for greatness. By raising and aiding a culture of support, encouragement and belief in the potential of others, we can create a ripple effect of positivity and motivation that propels individuals, especially our women, to reach their full potential.

Acknowledging and celebrating the progress and success of others is a powerful way to uplift and motivate them to continue striving for enormity. By recognising their efforts and achievements, we reinforce their confidence, boost their morale and inspire them to set even higher goals for themselves. We should aim to create a world where everyone has the opportunity to shine brightly.

Chapter 10

Gents...Time to Rip That Plaster Off!

I t's all about overcoming discrimination in the Modern Age.

Today, we are living in an interconnected world where diversity is celebrated and inclusion is championed, and still, it is disheartening to acknowledge that prejudices still linger in various forms. However, it is crucial to recognise that despite this ghastliness, we must continue to stand together as individuals and communities in order to overcome these unfriendly aggressions.

One of the first steps is to acknowledge its existence and aim to work with grassroots movements, social media campaigns and community organisations. The key is to create inclusive spaces where all individuals feel welcome and accepted, whether this is through mentorship, allyship, or providing resources and opportunities. Whatever it is, it is time to take a comprehensive approach and get rid of this long haul traditional discrimination from among us and finally set our women free.

The fact that these inequalities have existed for centuries, with historical records and evidence showing their presence in various cultures, means that this is outdated and should not be even recognised in this modern age. The extent and nature of these biases and unjust norms have varied across different time periods and regions. As far back as in many ancient civilizations, such as ancient Mesopotamia, Greece, Egypt and Rome, gender-based prejudices were prevalent. Women often had limited rights and opportunities compared to men and were typically subordinate in social, political and economic spheres. During the Middle Ages and the Renaissance, gender roles were often rigidly defined, with women largely confined to domestic roles and men holding power and authority in public life. The concept of male supremacy, where men held primary power and women were largely excluded from positions of influence, was the catalyst of where it was established.

However, the Industrial Revolution and subsequent modernisation of societies brought change to gender roles and inequalities. While women began to enter the workforce in larger numbers, they still faced discrimination, lower wages and limited opportunities for advancement compared to men. The 20th Century saw significant developments in the fight for gender equality, with movements such as first-wave feminism, second-wave feminism and subsequent waves working to challenge and dismantle this inequality. In many parts of the world, legal reforms, changes in social attitudes and increased awareness of gender issues have contributed to progress towards greater changes.

Despite these advancements, gender-based inequalities continue to persist in various forms today. Efforts to address and overcome this traditional narrow-mindedness remain ongoing. It's time to face the drums, rip that plaster off once and for all, and let it hurt. It is an insistent demand on us, that we consciously think about what we model and portray to our children and stop pouring lies and corrupt communications into the ears of our younger generation. We know very well that children learn a great deal by observing the behaviours and actions of those around them, particularly their parents, older siblings and influential figures in their lives. They often mimic the behaviours they see in adults and tend to believe what's impressed upon their minds. Our attitudes, values and beliefs are often passed down to children through modelling. So, it is important to be mindful of the messages we convey about respect and equality, and other values that we want to instil in our children. We must help them to develop a positive and open-minded attitude towards everyone, and that's why it is so important to show appreciation for diversity in all its forms. We have to be intentional about what we model and portray, so we can positively influence their development and help them grow into non-prejudiced, empathetic and responsible individuals.

As I have experienced firsthand, I can tell you that facing reality head-on is an essential part of life which boosts your personal growth and moves you forward. It can get tough, but it is often the first step towards positive change and self-empowerment. There are some key advantages of facing facts and truth if you approach things with an open mind. You get clarity and awareness, which helps you to gain a clearer understanding of yourself, the situations, as well as the world around you. It encourages self-reflection and introspection, and you learn from your own experiences. We become much more self-aware individuals, which will deepen connections and build stronger bonds with friends, loved ones and colleagues who we interact with daily. When we face up to reality, it helps us to identify and address problems more effectively. We develop realistic strategies and solutions to overcome obstacles and achieve our goals. A lot of times, the truth leads to emotional healing when we accept the facts of the situation, and that in itself allows us to process our feelings sincerely, as well as experience a sense of relief, closure and inner peace. Facing and confronting realities enables us to override setbacks, disappointments, and uncertainties with greater strength and confidence. I believe that living in alignment with the real world and the truth only promotes authenticity and integrity in how we live.

Overall, facing facts is a powerful and transformative process which have some key advantages, and we should indulge in this more often, especially towards our women. It is a vital step to understand and banish selfish behaviours and inequalities from within us and open that door to self-growth. When we are open and transparent, not just with ourselves but with others, it helps to build stronger and more legitimate connections.

By recognising these errant ways in us as men, we can significantly change the way we mistreat and degrade our highly valued women who are the matriarchs; the emotional and spiritual centre of the family. They are the keepers of family history, stories and traditions, ensuring that the family's legacy is passed down and preserved for future generations. They serve as powerful role models for young people, demonstrating strength, perseverance and compassion. She is the importance of family bonds.

We should honour her contributions and strengthen those bonds that hold families together across generations, and I am unapologetic in pushing these views forward because I know that gender equality is a fundamental human right that benefits society as a whole. It is important that men do actively support and speak out against the maltreatment of our women because we have a unique opportunity to influence other men and challenge the so-called gender norms which have been nothing but cold and brutal for centuries to our women. Our mothers have endured so many restrictive and damaging clichés, ruthless domestic violence and toxic behaviour by men.

I sincerely wish that more men would be steadfast in demonstrating a firm stance on promoting respect for women by educating themselves on the impact of sexism and discrimination and becoming more informed and empathetic on gender issues. Some of the contributory factors that continue to preserve and uphold these dogmatisms are too many sexist jokes, comments and phrases that carry sinister undertones against women, which are too often easily blurted out and overlooked, both in personal lives and larger societal contexts. This helps to create a culture of less mutual respect and self-pride for our women.

Concrete actions should be taken against sexist behaviours, especially by men, to eradicate chauvinistic ideologies and create a safer, more respectful environment where everyone can enjoy social equality regardless of gender. It is crucial to establish a zero-tolerance policy towards any form of sexism, as it not only violates basic human rights but also undermines the principles of manners and respect.

It must be said, that when encountering instances of sexist behaviour in any form, it is important to address them promptly and decisively. Opening communication about the issue straight away, along with clear guidelines on what is acceptable behaviour, is key to setting the tone for a respectful community. We ought to lead by example and consistently demonstrate our commitment to gender equality and hold individuals accountable for their actions. As soon as these cases are identified, then swift and appropriate action must be taken, as this is the only path to break the cycle. It is important also to ensure that the consequences are proportionate to the offense and serve as a deterrent to prevent future occurrences. We must provide support to women who are victims of sexist behaviour, create avenues for reporting incidents and offer counselling services to them when needed. Ultimately, to combat this behaviour requires a collective effort from all members of the community, but especially from men.

Chapter 11

Women Shaping The Future

W ell…there's a lot to showcase when it comes to visions and innovations concerning women. It's just a matter of where to begin! I think I will start with pioneering women in technology.

Men have made significant contributions to the tech industry, and so do our women. It was estimated on the 27th of May 2024, according to an update on Women in Tech Statistics by Luisa Zhou, that women only represent 33% of the workforce at large tech companies. This figure shows that women are advancing steadily but still not enough in technology-related careers, and the main reason for this is due to the lack of female role models within the technological sector. This is mainly because of the gender stereotypes of men being better at maths and science which is simply not true.

Here we have 7 of the most influential women in technology, namely: Ada Lovelace, Grace Hopper, Katherine Johnson, Annie Easley,

Margaret Hamilton, Adele Goldberg and Radia Perlman among others. It is evident that the world has made notable progress in this field but a lot more is still required.

Let's take a look at Ada Lovelace. Her full name was Augusta Ada King, Countess of Lovelace, born on 10th December 1815 and died on 27th November 1852. She was an English mathematician and writer, chiefly known for her work on Charles Babbage's early mechanical general-purpose computer, the Analytical Engine. Her notes on the engine include what is now considered to be the first algorithm intended to be processed by a machine, making her the world's first computer programmer. Ada Lovelace's work and contributions to the field of computer science have led to her often being regarded as the first computer programmer in history. She was a visionary thinker who demonstrated remarkable foresight in her writings about the Analytical Engine. She envisioned the machine being used for a wide range of applications beyond mere number crunching, including creating music and art. Her visionary thinking was well ahead of her time and has since been proven to be incredibly prescient, clearly knowing coming events.

Let's put the spotlight now on Grace Hopper. Hopper was born Grace Brewster Murray Hopper on the 9th of December 1906. She was also a pioneering computer scientist and United States Navy rear admiral. She was one of the first programmers of the Harvard Mark I computer and is credited with popularising the idea of machine-independent programming languages, leading to the development of COBOL (Common Business-Oriented Language). Throughout her career, Grace made significant contributions to the field of computer science and technology. Some of her notable achievements include Programming, as she was a key figure in the development of early computers and programming languages. She developed the first compiler for a computer programming language, which eventually led to the creation of COBOL, a language still in use today.

Let's turn our attention to another magnificently impressive female, Katherine Johnson.

Katherine was an African American mathematician whose calculations were critical to the success of NASA's early human spaceflight missions. She worked for NASA from 1953 until her retirement in 1986. Katherine's work was instrumental in Alan Shepard's 1961 Freedom 7 mission, which was the first American human spaceflight. She also played a key role in John Glenn's historic orbital flight aboard Friendship 7 in 1962. Johnson's contributions were featured in the book "Hidden Figures" by Margot Lee Shetterly, which was later adapted into a film of the same name. The book and the film brought attention to the important work done by Katherine Johnson and other African American women mathematicians at NASA during the early days of the space program. She was seen as the human-computer. Her precise calculations and analytical skills were crucial to the success of several key missions.

She overcame racial and gender barriers to become a respected and trailblazing figure in the fields of mathematics and aerospace engineering.

Another strong and outstanding African American computer scientist, mathematician, and rocket scientist who worked also for the National Aeronautics and Space Administration (NASA), was Annie Easley. She is known for her pioneering work in developing software for the Centaur rocket stage, as well as for her contributions to the advancement of computer technology and energy conversion systems.

Easley began her career at NASA in 1955 as a "human computer" like Katherine, performing complex mathematical calculations by hand. Over the years, she transitioned to programming and software development, working on a variety of projects that were critical to the success of numerous space missions. One of Easley's most notable achievements was her work on the Centaur rocket, where she developed and implemented software that was instrumental in optimising the rocket's performance and ensuring its reliability. Her work on the Centaur project played a key role in the success of various missions, including the Viking missions to Mars and the Voyager missions to the outer planets.

In addition to her technical contributions, Easley was also a strong advocate for equal opportunities in the field of STEM (science, technology, engineering, and mathematics). She faced discrimination and challenges as a woman of colour in a predominantly white and male-dominated field but persevered and made significant contributions that continue to inspire future generations of scientists and engineers.

Overall, Annie Easley's work exemplifies her dedication, innovation, and resilience in overcoming obstacles to make lasting contributions to the fields of computer science, mathematics, and aerospace engineering.

Now as we move to the TV screens, we look back on the immense work and vital contributions of Margaret Hamilton. Margaret Brainard Hamilton was an American actress best known for her iconic portrayal of the "Wicked Witch of the West" in the classic 1939 film "The Wizard of Oz." She was born on the 9th of December 1902 and passed away on the 16th of May 1985. Hamilton's performance as the Wicked Witch of the West remains one of the most memorable and enduring in film history; her cackling laugh, green makeup, and pointed hat have become iconic symbols of villainy in popular culture.

Aside from her role in "The Wizard of Oz," Hamilton, who was also a former school teacher, had a long and successful career as a character actress in film, television, and on stage. She appeared in numerous films and TV shows throughout the 1930s, 1940s, and 1950s, often playing comedic or villainous roles. Margaret Hamilton's contribution to the entertainment industry and her unforgettable portrayal of the Wicked Witch of the West have solidified her place in Hollywood's history. She also gained recognition for her work as an advocate of causes designed to benefit children and animals and retained a lifelong commitment to public education.

On the 22nd July 1945, the earth was gifted with yet another prominent American computer scientist, known for her significant contributions to the field of computer science, particularly in the area of programming languages and software engineering, Dr Adele Goldberg.

Goldberg's most notable contribution is her work on the development of the programming language Smalltalk. Smalltalk is an influential object-oriented programming language that has had a major impact on the field of software development. Dr Goldberg played a key role in the design and implementation of Smalltalk, helping to shape the way that object-oriented programming is practised today.

In addition to her work on Smalltalk, Goldberg has also made important contributions to the field of software engineering, particularly in the areas of user interface design and software development methodologies. Her research has helped to advance the understanding of how to design and build software systems that are both effective and easy to use. Overall, Dr Adele Goldberg's contributions to computer science have had a lasting impact on the field, and she is widely recognized for her expertise and innovation in programming languages and software engineering.

Radia Perlman! If you haven't heard this name before, then you need to research and delve deeper. She has earned the nickname "Mother of the Internet" for a valid, good reason.

Born on the 18th of December 1951, Radia Joy Perlman is a software designer and network engineer known for her significant contributions to the field of computer networking. She is a major figure in assembling the networks and technology that enable what we now know as the Internet. She is most famous for inventing the Spanning Tree Protocol (STP), which is a crucial algorithm that enables network bridges to work efficiently without causing loops in Ethernet networks. Perlman also designed the TRILL (Transparent Interconnection of Lots of Links) protocol, which is an improvement over STP and aims to provide faster and more efficient Ethernet networks. Additionally, she has made contributions to other areas of network design and security.

Aside from her technical achievements, Radia Perlman has also written a book called "Interconnections: Bridges, Routers, Switches, and Internetworking Protocols," which is considered a classic in the field of networking. She has received numerous awards for her work, including inductions into the Internet Hall of Fame and the National Academy of Engineering.

These are just a few examples of the many women who have made significant contributions to technology and paved the way for future generations of women in the field. Their achievements have been instrumental in shaping the technological landscape we see today.

Hedy Lamarr, Jean E. Sammet and Susan Kare are all among the inventors and co-developers who either laid the foundations themselves or contributed substantially to the tech development in the industry we know today.

Let us celebrate our remarkable women who have tirelessly dedicated themselves to constructing the panorama of technology. We not only honour their achievements but also recognize the collective impact of their pioneering spirit. As we commend these trailblazers for their innovation, resilience, and unwavering commitment to excellence, let us be inspired by their stories and let their successes serve as a beacon of hope and empowerment for aspiring women in tech everywhere. Together, let us continue to champion diversity, equality, and inclusivity, not only in the tech industry but in our everyday lives, ensuring that the voices and talents of all individuals are heard and valued.

I would just like to finish this chapter with the story of one remarkable, outstanding lady called Marie.

In the annals of scientific history, there are exceptional women whose groundbreaking discoveries have reshaped our understanding of the world. Among these trailblazers stands Marie Curie, a pioneering physicist and chemist known for her groundbreaking research on radioactivity. Her unparalleled contributions to science and technology have left an indelible mark on the fields of physics and chemistry, inspiring generations of women to pursue careers in STEM disciplines.

Born in Warsaw, Poland in 1867, Marie Curie (née Skłodowska) displayed a keen interest in science from a young age. Despite facing gender-based barriers to education, she overcame societal norms and went on to study physics and mathematics at the Sorbonne in Paris. It was there that she met Pierre Curie, a fellow scientist with whom she would form a lifelong partnership in both marriage and scientific collaboration. Marie Curie's most significant discovery came in 1898 when she and Pierre isolated the radioactive elements polonium and radium. This groundbreaking work not only revolutionized the field of chemistry, but also laid the foundation for the development of modern nuclear physics. In 1903, Marie Curie became the first woman to win a Nobel Prize, jointly awarded with Pierre and physicist Henri Becquerel for their research on radioactivity.

Marie Curie's pioneering research in radioactivity not only earned her a second Nobel Prize in Chemistry in 1911, but also established her as a trendsetter in the male-dominated world of science. Her tireless dedication to scientific inquiry and her unwavering commitment to advancing knowledge have inspired countless women to pursue careers in science and technology, paving the way for future generations of female scientists.

More than a century after her groundbreaking discoveries, Marie Curie's legacy continues to inspire and empower women in the fields of science and technology. Her remarkable achievements serve as a testament to the power of perseverance, intellect, and passion in overcoming obstacles and driving meaningful change in the world. Marie Curie's legacy as one of the greatest women in science and technology is a testament to the transformative impact of female leadership and innovation. Her pioneering spirit, coupled with her groundbreaking discoveries, has not only advanced the frontiers of scientific knowledge but has also shattered and melted iron barriers, opening doors for women in STEM fields worldwide.

Today the future of technology is bright, and it is in the hands of these visionary women that we find the strength and inspiration to help build a more inclusive and innovative world for generations to come.

Chapter 12

Championing Social Justice

L et me start by explaining what social justice is to me.

To me, it is the backbone of the morals in society. It encircles fair and equitable opportunities and the rights within communities. It involves addressing and rectifying systemic inequalities and injustices, which exist based on factors such as race, gender, sexual orientation, socioeconomic status, disability, and more.

With that said, social justice aims to ensure that all individuals have equal access to basic human rights in terms of education, healthcare, housing, employment and equal distribution of resources. It also involves weeding out the discriminatory practices and structures against women that continue to preserve inequality and marginalization. I'm convinced that we as a society will not be content until we take full control of all human rights violations, which mean strategies for creating meaningful change should be active and strongly implemented.

Throughout history, as we have emphasized enormously throughout this literature, our women have often been the victims of social injustices. They've been at the forefront of protest and gatherings such as the suffrage movement, civil rights and environmental justice movements and much more. They have worked tirelessly to challenge unfavourable laws and practices, raise awareness about issues affecting disempowered communities and push for systemic change, and indeed there is still much more work to be done in addressing the ways in which we tackle this difficult conundrum.

Efforts to address these challenges require a multifaceted approach. It is crucial to advocate for stronger laws and policies that protect women's rights and ensure gender equality. Additionally, raising awareness about the issues are essential steps in creating a more just and prosperous life for all of us irrespective of being a man or a woman. It is important to support the voices of women who are working to address these issues. This includes listening to and amplifying their experiences of discreditation and creating spaces for women to advocate for themselves and their communities.

We (men) should recognise the ways in which women are disproportionately affected by social injustice and use our platforms and privileges to speak out against it. We should endorse equal opportunities and support policies and initiatives that aim to level the playing field for all genders. We should certainly make a conscious effort to change the behaviour and structures of gender harassment in our world. After all, men and women have coexisted for centuries and both genders bring unique perspectives, strengths, and qualities to the table. We were created to inhabit, share and perform our duty of services to the planet. And therefore, societies will thrive when both genders are valued and respected and given equal opportunities.

By promoting impartiality and fairness between men and women, we can build a more sustainable future where everyone has the opportunity to reach their highest capability. We should respect each other's differences and work together, celebrating each other's strengths, so we can create a more peaceful balance and prosperous world for all to achieve great things. We are compromising our happiness each time we avail ourselves to discrimination, and then we suffer the negative impact. There are damaging consequences to situations when individuals and society allow them to persist.

Creating tension and animosity between different groups, kicks off social division and conflict, where inevitably it results in the breakdown of social cohesion and trust. This can also have diminished individual potential, serious economic repercussion and significant psychological harm that triggers the negative impact, leading straight to the mental health breakdowns and the well-being of people.

This undermines major facets of our human rights and shrinks the fundamental dignity and respect for all persons. We should always be on the lookout for any threats that target the stifling of diversity and inclusion. One of the craftiest little stereotypes which is common in diversity but not apparent, is what's known as Tokenism. You'll find this more commonly operating in the work environment. This occurs when individuals from underrepresented groups are included, merely to give the appearance of diversity, without being given meaningful opportunities for growth and advancement. This is a symbolic gesture to deflect criticism, which you will come across as I've said in many of our employment settings, and it is not hard to spot the true intentions of their desired goal. What I want to say is, if it's not coming from your heart, it's not gonna work. Just take a look at some of the insincerity and ineffectiveness of the tokenistic practices. First, they set up an illusion of inclusion which carries in it all the hollow promises that stands as a facade of progress, but it is in fact masking the underlying issues it purports to address. Despite its outward appearance of inclusivity, tokenism ultimately falls short in fostering real change and equality within a lot of organisations. This insidious practice, rooted in superficial gestures and symbolic representation, serves to fuel the very problems it claims to solve.

At its core, this is a strategy where one should be vigilantly guarded against when it is deployed, because by tokenizing individuals from underrepresented groups, these organisations seek to present a thin layer of progressiveness while avoiding meaningful structural change. So, these token efforts do little to address the systemic barriers and biases that hinder true diversity and inclusion. If we truly want social justice, we have to stop playing these games. Organisations must move beyond these double standard practices and embrace a genuine commitment to equity, representation, and inclusivity. We will be exactly where we are now, decades to come, if we fail to address the root causes of inequality and discrimination.

Only by challenging these existing power structures and promoting authentic diversity can organisations break free from the illusions of tokenism and build a truly inclusive environment for all communities on this planet, and not just hiding behind these surface-level gestures to fool people into thinking that they're trying to make meaningful changes.

The people who are mostly hurt in this gesture are the ones that have been tokenized and are led to believe that the institution they represent is genuinely thriving for an equitable and fair working environment, when in fact it was only half-heartedly done, to create a superficial diversity. It must be noted that this practice of Tokenism can be done for various reasons: some may do it to meet diversity quotas or to improve the organisation's image without making purposeful changes to promote inclusion. Some may engage in it to avoid criticism or accusations of discrimination, or in some cases, it can be used in the form of a box-ticking mentality, like a checkbox exercise to fulfil diversity requirements without a genuine commitment to diversity, and inclusion.

Having a few token individuals in an organisation can be a defense against claims of bias or lack of diversity. This can also be used to maintain existing power dynamics and hierarchies within an organisation. By tokenizing individuals from marginalised groups, the organisation can continue to prioritise the perspectives and interests of the dominant group without challenging the status quo. Consequently, the burden of this practice in the end often mentally presses on these tokenized individuals, where they find themselves isolated, unsupported and undervalued within the organisations, holding feelings of alienation and disempowerment that drags the weaker ones down.

In reality, Tokenism is a permeating issue that plagues many aspects of society, from workplaces to media representations, etc. It is a superficial and often a performative effort to promote diversity and inclusion to give the appearance of equality, while in reality, these individuals are often disempowered and not given equal opportunities or recognition.

One of the most insidious aspects of this issue that I dread is, it can actually fester the very inequalities it seeks to address. This not only undermines the value of their contributions but also reinforces the very stereotypical double standards it seeks to destroy initially. It can create an ulcer within the workforce that produces a toxic environment where individuals feel like they are not judged on their merits but on their demographic characteristics. This can lead to feelings of imposter syndrome, burnout, and ultimately hinder their professional growth and well-being.

When you look at media and entertainment, tokenism can manifest in the form of token characters who are included solely for the purpose of diversity quotas, rather than being fully developed and complex individuals. These characters often serve as averages or tropes, reinforcing harmful narratives and limiting the representation of diverse experiences.

Overall, the evil impact of tokenism lies in its continuation of inequality, its erasure of individuality and its failure to address the root causes of discrimination. To combat tokenism, it is essential to move beyond symbolic gestures and instead prioritise genuine inclusivity, equity and empowerment for all individuals, regardless of who they are and where they are from. We have to challenge tokenism and strive for true diversity and equality where we can manifest a more comprehensive unity for everyone no matter who they are.

Chapter 13

Sisterhood: Resilience And Strength

Sisterhood is a term used to describe the special bond and comradeship shared between women. It transcends blood relations and mere friendships and encompasses a deep sense of connection, support, and solidarity among women. It is a network of empathy that provides strength, trust and empowerment.

This powerful bond fosters a sense of belonging and community, creating a safe space where women can express themselves freely, share their experiences and uplift each other. The power of sisterhood lies in its ability to break down barriers, challenge generalisations and promote diversity. It encourages collaboration rather than competition, nurturing a culture of support and unity among women from different backgrounds, cultures and perspectives. The function of this network allows women to find encouragement to pursue their goals, overcome challenges and celebrate their achievements together.

So, Sisterhood is not just about shared experiences; it is also about collective action and advocacy for women's rights and equality, where women can expand their voices, stand up against injustice, and work towards creating a more balanced and interconnected world. It serves women as a source of persistency and inspiration among themselves.

By coming together, women can harness their collective power to effect positive change and build a more equal and supportive society that goes beyond boundaries. There is always a feeling of strong togetherness and love in sisterhood. It is built on a foundation of mutual respect and devotion. Women who uplift and empower each other create a positive and nurturing environment where they can thrive, grow and come together through common interests, passions or values. Whether it's a shared hobby, cause, or belief; having common ground helps them to integrate and create a sense of belonging. Sisterhood also involves a deep emotional connection where women feel comfortable expressing their thoughts, feelings and vulnerabilities. This emotional intimacy fosters trust and openness, allowing women to support each other through life's ups and downs. Overall, it is a bond that celebrates the uniqueness and strength of women.

The difference I find between sisterhood and brotherhood is, while brotherhood can bring about a sense of camaraderie, support, and solidarity among men just like sisterhood does, there can also be potential negatives and drawbacks associated with this concept. This includes, as in some brotherhood cases, the reinforcement of toxic masculinity such as aggression and the suppression of emotions. This creates pressure on men to conform to narrow preconceptions of masculinity and may discourage vulnerability or seeking help when we need it most.

Another harmful thing that is sometimes promoted is exclusivity, creating an in-group/ out-group dynamic leading to different cliques, where discrimination or marginalisation of individuals who do not fit into the established norms or expectations of the brotherhood group gets targeted. So, it becomes what is known as a groupthink, where individual members prioritise group consensus over critical thinking or independent decision-making. This can stifle creativity and alteration and even diversity of thought within the group, which can limit opportunities for learning, growth and understanding of different viewpoints.

One other thing that is noted within the brotherhood groups is the Pressure to Conform. There may be tensions for members to adapt to certain behaviours, beliefs, or values in order to fit in or gain acceptance. This can be restrictive and may prevent individuals from expressing their true self or pursuing their own interests while being a group member.

It can inadvertently enable, or reinforce, negative behaviours or risky decision-making through a culture of acceptance where normalisation is active within the group.

It is imperative however, that we build a positive brotherhood in today's society, as the concept of brotherhood among men holds significant importance. Negative behaviours and attitudes can erode the foundation of these relationships, leading to conflicts and misunderstandings. It is crucial for men to take proactive steps to stop and change the negative tide in brotherhood and thrive for a culture of respect, support and equitable fellowship within their groups. This can happen through honest and transparent conversations, where we can address underlying issues without fear of judgement and prevent misinterpretations from escalating.

One of the fundamental pillars of a healthy brotherhood is Respect. Emphasising the importance of treating each other with dignity, actively listening and showing empathy can be the magic wand to cultivate that culture of understanding. By acknowledging and valuing each other's perspectives, men can build stronger bonds based on trust and appreciation.

Overall, while sisterhood and brotherhood both involve bonds and relationships between individuals of the same gender, the specific dynamics, communication styles, socialization processes and shared experiences within these groups can vary exceptionally, based on societal expectations and individual personalities.

In conclusion, my journey of understanding and appreciating the values of sisterhood in our society as a man has been a transformative and enlightening experience. Through witnessing the bonds of sisterhood among the women in my life and the broader community, I have come to recognise the profound impact of these relationships on shaping a more integrated, empathetic and supportive society. As I reflect on the bonds I shared with my sisters Sharon, Leanora and Marcia, and the collective experiences we had growing up together (with me as the only boy), it reminds and inspires me of the strength and rebounding skills that women exhibit when they come together to uplift and support one another. The sense of community, understanding and oneness that define sisterhood serves as a powerful example of how individuals can forge meaningful connections and create positive change in our world.

I am committed to being an ally and advocate for the values of sisterhood, recognising the importance of amplifying women's voices, championing gender equality and harnessing a culture of harmony and solidarity. I believe that by standing together with my sisters and embracing the principles of sisterhood, we can work together to challenge harmful clichés, pull apart barriers to progress, and create good living for all, despite living in a world where gender norms and expectations often limit the full potential of individuals. As a man who appreciates and values the contributions of women in society, I am committed to standing alongside our women globally in the pursuit of a more compassionate, equal and harmonious world.

Together, let us continue to celebrate the strength and unity that sisterhood embodies, and strive towards a future where all individuals are empowered to thrive and succeed, irrespective of who you are. By honouring and upholding the values of sisterhood, we not only enrich our own lives but contribute to a more appealing society for the future generations.

Chapter 14

Who Gave Men The Right In The First Place?

L et me make this quite clear before I continue. You won't convince me that it was God!

As I have aforementioned, when it comes to exploring the origins of male supremacy over women, you cannot assess it without delving into the historical and cultural contexts that have kept this social domination in existence for so long.

One of the key arguments used to support this chauvinistic practice is the idea of a divine sanction, where it is believed that men were granted authority over women by a higher power. This concept is deep-seated in many religious teachings, as there are verses and interpretations that have been used to justify the subjugation of women to men. It is believed that men are the leaders and protectors of women, and that women should be obedient and submissive to their male counterparts. As we've explored earlier in previous chapters, these beliefs have been reinforced over time through institutions of religion, cultural practices and customs. These were the traditional and accepted ways of behaviour in those days. But that was in those days!

However, in today's rapidly evolving society, it is paramount that we address and square up to this long-standing tradition of male bigotry and pull it apart from the root. This archaic notion which is deeply entrenched in many cultures and societies is the main engine revving up the prolongation of gender inequality that restricts the progress and liberty of women worldwide. Living with this imbalance of power as a society not only undermines the inherent dignity and rights of women, but also hinders the collective advancement of humanity in general.

It is high time we challenge and reject the opinion that men are inherently superior to women. By disallowing the traditional acceptance of male dominance, we pave the way for a more fair and all-inclusive world where individuals are valued for their competence and contributions rather than their genetical make up.

The mutual stance now taken by so many (which shows the growing recognition of the importance of gender coordination) is to equip our women with power in the world, giving her more opportunity for independent action, which is not only a matter of basic human rights but also a key driver of social and economic development. Numerous studies have shown that gender-diverse teams are more innovative and productive, and societies that invest in gender equality tend to be more prosperous and stable. In this modern era characterised by progress, equality and respect for human rights, there exists no valid justification for the enslavement of women by men. Today the principles of gender equalness and women's rights are widely recognised and advocated for. The subduing of women by men is not only morally unjustifiable but also fundamentally incompatible with the values of a fair and just society.

We are in an era of enlightenment and evolution, and there is no legitimate basis for men to repress or justify the subordination of women. I call on all men with the same like mindedness who unapologetically support, respect and have high admiration for females in our society, to challenge and dismantle the integrity and functioning of these oppressive structures that have kept women thwarted and broken for far too long. Together we join in brotherhood on the one platform as men of backbone and ethics, to echo our voices for the discontinuation of men repressing and keeping women in servitude in this day and age. We shall stand with our Empresses to remove all posing obstacles that are determined to retain this malignant mindset towards them.

In a world filled with diversity, it is often our differences that lead to misunderstandings, xenophobia and unfair treatment. In my opinion, embracing fairness is the pathway to a better life, so the sooner we shed our unfair mindset towards each other, the sooner we can pave the way for a more harmonious and fulfilling life on this earth. At the core of our crooked mindset lies ignorance, fear and a lack of empathy. When we judge others based on shallow opinions of their characteristics such as race and gender, we are not only continuing with our discrimination, but we are also poisoning our own happiness and development.

To rid ourselves of these unfair dispositions, we must first acknowledge its presence within us. We must confront our own biases, challenge our assumptions and strive to see the humanity in each and every individual. It is through learning, awareness, and open-mindedness that we can begin to destroy the barriers that divide us for so long.

By cultivating a culture of inclusion and love, it is not just us in this current era that will be benefitted, but more so for the future generations to flourish. Our children deserve to inherit a world where acceptance and understanding are the norm, not the exception. It is our duty as exiting generations to lay the groundwork for a better tomorrow by sowing seeds of growth, respect and compassion today.

Let us embark on this journey towards a more impartial and square society. Let us commit ourselves to unlearning old prejudices, embracing multiplicity and championing appropriateness in all aspects of our lives. For the sooner we get rid of this dishonourable mindset towards each other, the sooner we can enjoy a better life on this earth - a life filled with immense joy, harmony and boundless possibilities. No man was ever given the right to be superior over women by any higher power. Man has given this accolade to himself and claims divine rights to it. This is clear cut, and the human mind is intelligent to see right through that transparency in this current day.

It is time to hang up the gloves gentlemen and retire from this penis dictatorship.

Life overall is beautiful, but there's a problem on earth called **MAN**!

Chapter 15

The Price of Liberation!

S he broke a lot of barriers, that's for sure, but what a price she pays to reach there!

Let us unveil the invisible burdens on women in our society. The journey towards liberation for women has been paved with sacrifices and hidden costs that are not always visible to the naked eye. While the pursuit of equality, freedom and integrity is a noble endeavour, it comes at a price that many women are all too familiar with.

One of the most glaring costs of liberation for our women today, is that burden of societal expectations and judgments in order to achieve this so-called "Stamp of Approval" from society. As women strive to break free from traditional gender roles and stereotypes, they often face backlashes, criticisms and scrutiny from those who are uncomfortable with their newfound independence. The pressure to conform to societal norms while simultaneously challenging them, do take a toll on many women's mental and emotional well-being, leading to feelings of seclusion, self-doubt and guilt. Moreover, the quest for liberation often comes at the expense of personal relationships and social connections. Family members, friends and even romantic partners may struggle to accept and support a woman's journey towards empowerment because of the norms of society, leading to strained relationships and emotional distancing.

We have seen that the need to assert one's independence and autonomy can sometimes result in estrangement and loneliness, as women find themselves drifting into uncharted territory without the familiar support systems in place to back them up.

If we take a look at financial independence, this is another crucial aspect of women's liberation that comes with its own set of challenges. As women strive to shatter the glass ceiling and achieve economic equality, they often face wage disparities, limited opportunities for advancement and systemic barriers that hinder their progress in the workplace. The struggle for equal pay and fair treatment can be exhausting and demoralising, forcing women to work twice as hard to prove their worth in a male-dominated world.

Furthermore, the quest for liberation of women is often intertwined with the constant fear of adverse reactions, violence and brutal attacks of discrimination. Women who dare to speak out against injustices, advocate for their rights or challenge the status quo are frequently met with hostility, threats and intimidation. The very act of asserting one's authority and demanding equality can make women vulnerable to harassment, abuse and harm, both online and offline. She's often faced with a barrage of discrimination and derogatory insults. Online, they are subjected to vicious attacks, including sexist remarks, threats of violence and targeted harassment campaigns aimed at silencing their voices. These attacks are not limited to anonymous trolls but also come from well-known figures and organised groups. Furthermore, women are disproportionately affected by online abuse, with studies showing that they are more likely to receive violent and sexually explicit threats compared to their male counterparts. Offline, women speaking out face similar challenges, including being dismissed, belittled or even ostracized in their communities. This culture of silencing and discrediting women not only fuels gender hatred but also discourages others from speaking out, creating a chilling effect that stifles important conversations and progress towards a more fair and equal society.

It is fair to say, the price that women pay to get liberated in our society is multifaceted and profound. It incorporates not only the visible struggles and obstacles that they face in their expedition for equality and verification, but also the unseen afflictions of public presumptions and wranglings in relationships due to clear financial distinctions. There's always a constant threat of counterblast and repercussions when they come forward to stand up for equal gender-rights. Their journey is a very expensive pathway to freedom. Women around the world have shouldered heavy burdens of hardship that often go unnoticed and unappreciated. From fighting for basic human rights to challenging male chauvinism and traditional toxicity against their gender, women have had to swim around a treacherous path, filled with hurdles and provocations as the price of their freedom is often high, requiring them to sacrifice personal comfort, safety and sometimes even their lives. In many parts of the world, women who dare to speak up against injustice or demand equality are met with serious counteractions and violence. The simple act of stating their rights can lead to exclusion from their communities, loss of livelihood and even imprisonment. There's not one shred of doubt that a woman's journey to freedom is undeniably an expensive pathway, riddled with financial challenges that inhibited her progress and limit her opportunities to better herself. The emotional toll of directing her way in a world that poses constant threats to her well-being further adds to the cost of seeking freedom and autonomy.

This barbaric hardship that women face in the pursuit of freedom is not only external, but also internal. Many women grapple with self-doubt, fear, and the feeling of culpability as they challenge the traditional customs of society. The weight of breaking free from these traditional roles and conventional images can be overwhelming, leading to mental and emotional traumas that are often invisible to the outside world. But despite these challenges, our women continue to persevere in marching forward for freedom and equality. Their resilience, courage and unwavering determination serve as a beacon of hope for future generations, as this long and arduous journey is written all over the pages of history and is still being written as we speak.

She has fought tirelessly, facing countless hurdles and confrontations along the way. She fought for her right to have an education, the right to work and pursue careers of her own choice, the right to make decisions concerning her own body and the right to participate fully in political, social and economic life. These rights are essential not only for the well-being and sanctions of individual women, but also for the progress and prosperity of societies in this world. This invaluable price of freedom is measured in the innumerable sacrifices, struggles and victories that have shaped the course of their history.

As we reflect on the freedom and liberation for our women, let us honour the legacy of those who have come before us and recommit ourselves to the ongoing struggle for gender equality. Let us stand together in solidarity, united in our shared vision of a world where every woman and girl has the opportunity to live a life of dignity, equality and freedom. It is a price worth paying for the benefits of gender equality which is marked by acts of courage, resilience and unwavering determination. The sacrifices made have been immeasurable. This invaluable price of freedom for women cannot be overstated, as it represents the fundamental right to live life on one's own terms, free from oppression, discrimination and limitations.

It is essential for society to recognise and appreciate these women's sacrifices and struggles which they have endured in the pursuit of their rights and happiness. Knowing that the price of their liberation, as huge as it seems, is still a small one to pay for the priceless gift of freedom and self-determination.

I salute you all - The Incredible VAGINA PEOPLE!

9 781835 383872